Animal Neighbours

Fox

700030293131

Michael Leach

WAYLAND

WORCESTERSHIRE COUNTY COUNCIL	
313	
Bertrams	10.02.07
J599.775	£6.99
BV	

Animal Neighbours

Titles in this series:

Badger • Bat • Deer • Fox • Hare • Hedgehog
Mole • Mouse • Otter • Owl • Rat • Swallow

Conceived and produced for Hodder Wayland by

Nutshell MEDIA

Intergen House, 65–67 Western Road, Hove BN3 2JQ, UK
www.nutshellmedialtd.co.uk

Commissioning Editor: Victoria Brooker
Editor: Polly Goodman
Designer: Tim Mayer
Illustrator: Jackie Harland

Published in Great Britain in 2003 by Hodder Wayland, an imprint of Hodder Children's Books.
Reprinted in 2004
This paperback edition published in 2007 by Wayland, an imprint of Hachette Children's Books
© Copyright 2003 Wayland

All rights reserved. Apart from any use permitted under UK copyright law, this publication may only be reproduced, stored or transmitted, in any form, or by any means with prior permission in writing of the publishers or in the case of reprographic production in accordance with the terms of licences issued by the Copyright Licensing Agency.

British Library Cataloguing in Publication Data
Leach, Michael, 1954–
Fox. – (Animal neighbours)
1. Foxes – Juvenile literature
I. Title
599.7'75

ISBN-10: 0 7502 5081 X
ISBN-13: 978 0 7502 5081 8

Printed and bound in Hong Kong

Hachette Children's Books
338 Euston Road, London NW1 3BH

Cover photograph: A female red fox walking in the Camargue, southern France.
Title page: A European red fox yawning.

Picture acknowledgements
FLPA 8 (W. L. Miller), 9 (Roger Tidman), 12 (Martin H. Smith), 23 (David T. Grewcock), 28 top (W. L. Miller), 28 right (Roger Tidman), 28 bottom left (Martin H. Smith), 28 top left (David T. Grewcock); Michael Leach 15, 20, 25; NHPA *Cover* (Hellio & Van Ingen), *Title page* (Mike Lane), 6–7 (Daryl Balfour), 6 (top) Andy Rouse, 10 (Manfred Danegger), 13 (Mike Lane), 14 (Andy Rouse), 17 (Daniel Heuchlin), 18–19 (Suzanne Danegger), 22 (Manfred Danegger), 24 (Stephen Dalton), 21 (Andy Rouse); Oxford Scientific Films 11, 21 (Mark Hamblin), 26 (Alan & Sandy Carey).

Contents

Meet the Fox   4

The Dog Family   6

Birth and Growing Up   8

Habitat   12

Food and Hunting   16

Finding a Mate   22

Threats   24

Fox Life Cycle   28

Fox Clues   29

Glossary   30

Finding Out More   31

Index   32

Meet the Fox

Thc fox is a bushy tailed member of the dog family. There are 12 species of true foxes, including the Arctic fox, the grey fox, and the red fox.

Foxes live throughout the world, except in Antarctica and South-east Asia. They can be found in forests, farmland and deserts, and in many cities and suburbs. This book looks at the red fox – the most widespread species in the world.

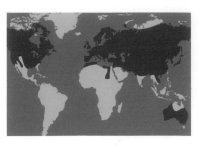

▲ The red shading on this map shows where red foxes live in the world today.

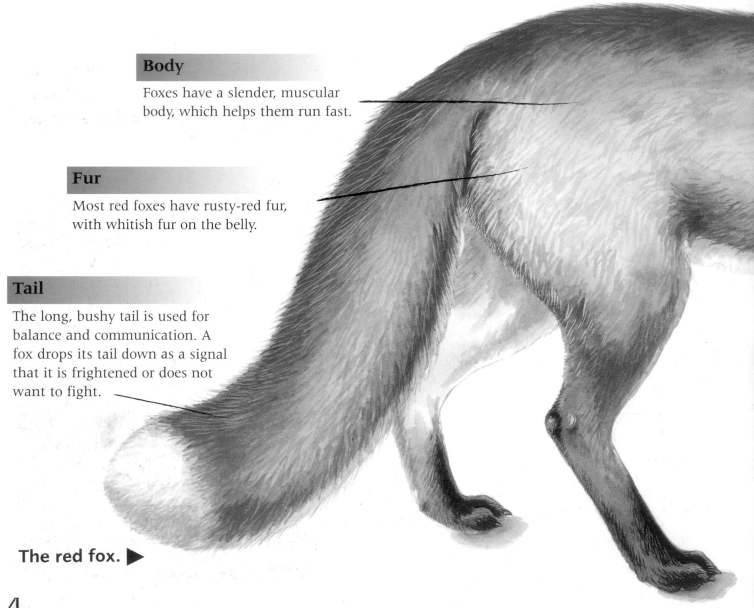

Body
Foxes have a slender, muscular body, which helps them run fast.

Fur
Most red foxes have rusty-red fur, with whitish fur on the belly.

Tail
The long, bushy tail is used for balance and communication. A fox drops its tail down as a signal that it is frightened or does not want to fight.

The red fox. ▶

4

Ears

Foxes have an excellent sense of hearing, which they use to track down their prey.

Eyes

The fox's eyes are large and forward-facing, which helps it spot its prey.

Teeth

Sharp, pointed canine teeth help rip into the flesh of prey.

◀ The red fox is larger than a domestic cat.

Legs

Long legs help the fox run fast when chasing its prey.

Claws

Unlike cats, the claws of foxes are non-retractable, which helps them grip the ground when they are running.

FOX FACTS

The red fox's scientific name is *Vulpes vulpes*, which comes from the Latin word *vulpinus*, meaning 'cunning'.

Male foxes are known as dogs, females are vixens and young foxes are cubs.

Red foxes measure up to 70 cm long excluding the tail, and up to 40 cm tall at the shoulder. The tail can be as long as 49 cm.

Males weigh an average of 6.7 kg. Females weigh an average of 5.4 kg.

The Dog Family

There are 35 species in the dog family. All dogs are predators – hunters that kill other animals for food. The largest member of the dog family is the grey wolf. This tall, powerful creature is strong enough to kill a fully grown deer.

Not all dogs hunt big animals. The tiny bat-eared fox in Africa lives mainly on insects and earthworms.

The grey wolf lives ▶ in Europe, North America and Asia.

Wild dogs are well adapted to living in different habitats. The Arctic fox has a thick coat of fur, which protects it from below-freezing temperatures of -40 °C.

The fennec fox has the opposite problem to the Arctic fox. It lives in the Sahara Desert. To avoid the hot sun, this fox comes out only at night. Its huge ears help to keep it cool by releasing body heat. They also give the fox excellent hearing, which helps it detect its prey.

▼ Bat-eared foxes are nocturnal hunters. Their huge ears pick up sounds of small animals moving around in the dark.

FIRST PETS

About 20,000 years ago, wild wolf cubs were captured and tamed by humans. Since then, individuals have been selected and bred to produce a huge range of different sizes and colours. These are the pet dogs that now share our homes.

Birth and Growing Up

It is springtime, and a heavily pregnant vixen looks for a den, or 'earth', to have her cubs. This could be a new tunnel that she digs, or an old hole made by badgers or other animals. In towns and cities, she might make an earth on a roadside verge, next to a railway line, or even in someone's garden.

At birth, the cubs are completely blind and deaf, born with their eyes and ears tightly closed. The one good sense they have is of smell. When they are about 10 days old, their eyes and ears slowly open.

▲ These new-born fox cubs huddle together to keep warm while their mother is out hunting.

Unless she is out hunting, the mother stays with her litter most of the time, allowing them to suckle several times a day. If the earth is disturbed by people, dogs or other enemies, the vixen will carry the cubs to a safer place up to 1 kilometre away. When the cubs are 3 weeks old, the vixen starts to leave the earth for longer periods of time.

FOX CUBS

New-born fox cubs are about 10 cm long and weigh about 110 g.

A vixen normally gives birth to a litter of between four and eight cubs, but as many as 12 have been recorded.

▼ Fox cubs carefully sniff the air for danger before moving out of the earth's entrance.

Early days

The cubs first leave the earth at around 30 days old. This is also when they begin to eat solid food. Their mother carries meat to the earth in her stomach. As soon as they see her, the cubs start to beg. As their mother coughs up the meat, the cubs gulp it as quickly as possible.

▼ A vixen feeds her hungry cub by passing food to it through her mouth. The partly digested food is easy for the cub to digest.

FOX CALLS

Foxes communicate with scent, sound and body language. They can produce 28 different calls, each with its own meaning. A short, loud yap shows anger, a long yelp attracts a mate, and vixens use a soft whine to communicate with their cubs.

Cubs spend their early days close to the earth's entrance, quickly disappearing underground if danger threatens. On warm days they laze about in the sun. They spend a lot of time play-fighting with each other, digging and playing games with sticks, bones and anything else lying near the earth. These games strengthen the cubs' muscles and teach them the basic skills of hunting.

By the autumn, the cubs are 8 months old and almost fully grown. One by one, the young foxes leave their mother and become independent. By the end of the year, they will all have gone.

▲ Fox cubs have such sharp teeth that they can injure each other when they are play-fighting.

Habitat

▲ These two foxes are about to fight over territory. Such fights are noisy and dramatic.

After leaving their mother, the young foxes must find their own territory. Each fox needs an area that provides plenty of food and shelter, and is not already home to any other fox. Every year, young foxes from many different litters compete for territories.

The strongest foxes win the best hunting grounds. The other youngsters may have to look for longer, but it won't be hard to find their own territory because red foxes live in such a wide range of habitats. They can make their home in woodlands, farmland, towns, rubbish tips and almost any other habitat. Once a fox has found a good territory, it stays there for life.

Each fox marks its territory with droppings and urine carefully left on stones and logs. This is called scent-marking. The scents are powerful smell signals that warn other foxes to keep away.

▼ A fox marks its territory with a spray of urine that will smell for up to two days.

TERRITORY

A fox's territory can be up to 20 square kilometres.

Dogs usually have larger territories than vixens.

Fox territories sometimes slightly overlap, but neighbouring foxes always try to avoid each other.

Town and country

The red fox's rusty coat is perfect camouflage in a woodland at night, keeping it well hidden as it stalks through leaves and undergrowth. But in other habitats, its colouring is less useful. Foxes living in towns and cities can be very easy to see against a background of tarmac and concrete.

▼ **Foxes were originally animals of the forest. They have moved to other habitats because many woodlands have been destroyed by humans.**

Most urban foxes have never been in a forest or a field. Their behaviour is suited to the urban habitat. Urban foxes stay hidden during the day, sleeping in abandoned buildings, underneath bushes and even on roofs. They do not come out until dark, when most people have gone inside. Unlike urban foxes, rural foxes often hunt in the daylight, especially in winter, when food is hard to find.

COOL FOXES

Red foxes living in northern Europe and Canada are specially adapted to their cool climate. Apart from having thicker fur than foxes living in warmer habitats, they are also not as tall. Long legs lose more heat than shorter legs, so their short legs help to keep them warm.

▼ **Urban foxes find food in unusual places. A good sense of smell allowed this fox to find scraps of food on a bird table.**

Food and Hunting

Foxes are omnivores. They eat worms, insects, voles, mice, rabbits and a wide variety of other small animals, as well as plant food such as grass and berries. Each adult fox eats about 500 grams of food a day. They need more food in winter to keep warm.

▼ Foxes are at the top of their food chain. Here is some of the food that foxes eat. (The illustrations are not to scale).

Fox food chain

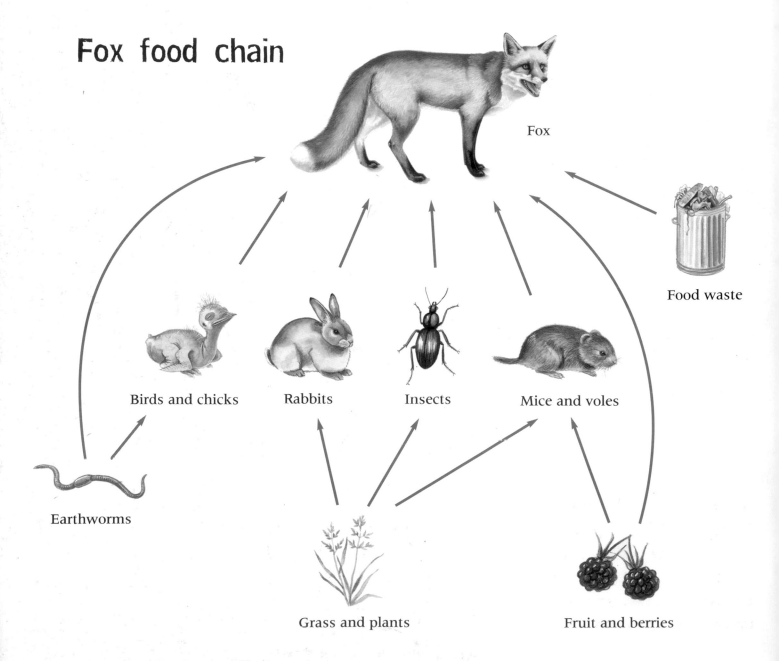

Fox

Food waste

Birds and chicks

Rabbits

Insects

Mice and voles

Earthworms

Grass and plants

Fruit and berries

The fox's diet changes throughout the year, according to the food available. In the spring, mice and voles are a source of food because it is their breeding season. As the young mice and voles leave their dens for the first time, they provide easy pickings for foxes.

In the autumn, foxes eat fruit and berries. During bad winter weather, they eat the bodies of animals that have died in the cold.

Foxes also raid birds' nests on the ground and in low bushes, eating the chicks or the eggs inside.

Some foxes raid farms ▶ to hunt chickens, geese or new-born lambs. If this becomes a habit, farmers can lose a lot of animals unless the fox is shot.

Hunting

The fox hunts mostly at night. It is a quick and
skilful hunter, using hearing, smell and sight
to find its prey. If its sensitive nose smells an
underground nest of mice or voles, the fox
will dig deep into the soil to reach it.

Foxes regularly search grassy meadows looking
for mice, frequently stopping to look and listen.
When they hear a rustle or see a slight movement
in the undergrowth, they jump and pin the
mouse to the ground with their front paws.

Foxes stalk bigger prey by silently creeping
forwards at first, trying to get as near
as possible before being noticed. At the
last minute they sprint and pounce,
immediately killing the animal with
their sharp teeth. Sometimes foxes
ambush mice or rabbits by lying
near a burrow and waiting for
them to appear.

▼ Foxes rely on surprise when hunting. A flock of fully grown geese can defend themselves against a fox only if they see it in time.

FOLK-TALE FOXES

In folk tales all around the world, foxes are portrayed as being clever, quick and cunning. In stories such as *Brer Rabbit* and *Aesop's Fables*, the fox is shown as a ruthless hunter that uses its intelligence to catch prey.

Storing food

Foxes usually eat their prey immediately, but after a big kill they may hide left-over meat. They dig a shallow hole in the ground with their front paws, drop in the meat and cover it with soil. They will come back to eat the food later. Storing food helps foxes survive days when there is little prey available, but other animals such as badgers often find and eat the food before the fox returns.

▼ **Urban foxes soon learn which rubbish bins are likely to contain the best food.**

FOX TRAVEL

The red fox was once found only in Europe. During the eighteenth and nineteenth centuries, when Europeans were settling in other continents, many foxes were captured and taken to the new settlements to help control the number of rats and mice there. Wild foxes now live and breed successfully in countries such as the USA, Canada and Australia.

Food in towns

Urban foxes are useful to humans because they keep down the number of rats and mice that live in built-up areas. But apart from eating rats and mice, urban foxes have learned to take advantage of people's wasteful habits. They raid dustbins and rubbish tips looking for bones, crusts and other food that we have thrown away. They visit waste bins outside fast-food shops looking for left-over chips and burgers.

Foxes are clever animals that know where to find easy meals. They steal dog and cat food from bowls and have even been seen entering kitchens to find food. All foxes will eat carrion, and they often search roadside verges, looking for the bodies of animals killed by traffic.

Foxes can be injured by tin ▶ cans and broken bottles when searching through rubbish.

Finding a Mate

After they are a year old, foxes are ready to breed. The mating season is in January and February each year. There is a period of only three days when the vixen can become pregnant.

▲ Fights between male foxes may look dangerous, but the weaker fox usually runs off before it is injured.

As this time approaches, the vixen attracts nearby males with a long, loud call. The call can be heard over $1/2$ kilometre away and several males usually respond.

When the males appear, they fight. The weaker males are driven away, leaving only the stronger, dominant fox to mate. He will stay with the vixen for a few days, before moving on to mate with one or two other females. About 55 days after mating, the new cubs are born.

▼ The vixen (below right) is often aggressive to the dog before she allows him to mate.

GHOSTLY CALL

Vixens looking for a mate give out loud, haunting squeals at night. In many countries, this sound was believed to be the cry of ghosts. Some people once thought it was a sign that a human was about to die.

Threats

Foxes can live to the age of 10 in the wild, but most die much younger. Urban foxes are sometimes killed by large dogs. Healthy adult foxes are too quick to be caught by most predators, but old, injured or sick foxes cannot run fast enough to get away.

In some countries, large predators such as bears dig up and eat fox cubs from their earths. In Europe, most large predators such as wolves and bears have been wiped out by humans over the last 200 years, so people are now the fox's greatest enemy.

FOX MYTHS

The Incas of South America worshipped the fox as a god. But Europeans in the Middle Ages believed that foxes were associated with the devil. Many foxes were destroyed because they were thought to attract evil spirits.

◀ This large retriever has just killed a fox. In Europe, foxes have been hunted by trained hounds for centuries.

Road traffic is the red fox's biggest killer. In Britain alone, around 20,000 foxes die on the roads every year. Similar numbers are killed in many other countries. About 90 per cent of foxes living in towns are hit by cars at least once during their life. Even if they are not killed, they may be badly injured. Town foxes can often survive their injuries by eating scraps of left-over food while they recover. But foxes in the countryside usually die after being injured because they cannot run and hunt.

▼ Urban foxes like this one show no fear of cars, so many are hit as they cross roads.

Friend or foe?

Some people in the countryside do not like foxes because they prey on chickens, geese and newborn lambs. Many farmers protect their livestock by killing foxes with traps, poisonous gas, shotguns, poisoned bait and hounds. However, foxes also help farmers by eating mice and rats, which eat cereal crops and stored grains. In some areas where foxes were killed off, rodents increased so much that farmers had to bring in more foxes to help get rid of them.

▲ Foxes that raid chicken sheds often kill more birds than they can eat.

People in towns often welcome foxes and give them food. They can become so tame that they will take meat directly from a person's hand. In some towns there are now more foxes per kilometre than in the surrounding countryside.

In many places, foxes are the main carriers of rabies. Millions of foxes have been killed in an attempt to stop this disease spreading, since it can affect humans as well as animals. Foxes can also suffer from other diseases such as distemper, which can wipe out large numbers very quickly.

▼ **Pet cats and wild foxes treat each other with suspicion. Both could be hurt if they fought.**

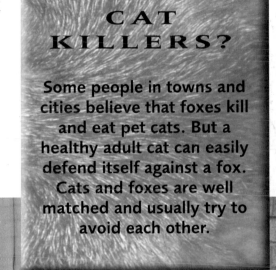

CAT KILLERS?

Some people in towns and cities believe that foxes kill and eat pet cats. But a healthy adult cat can easily defend itself against a fox. Cats and foxes are well matched and usually try to avoid each other.

Fox Life Cycle

1 The new-born fox cub is blind and weighs just 110 g. It is one of a litter of four to eight cubs.

2 Ten days after birth, the cub's eyes and ears open for the first time.

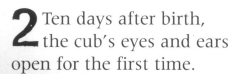

6 At the age of 12 months, the fox breeds for the first time.

3 At 1 month old, the cub leaves the earth for the first time and has its first taste of solid food.

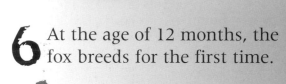

5 Each young fox wanders alone until it finds a suitable territory.

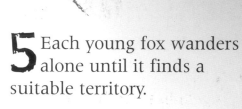

4 The cubs leave their mother in the autumn, at the age of around 6 months old.

Fox Clues

Look out for the following clues to help you find signs of a fox:

Earth
A single hole in the ground, or a burrow beneath a shed or other building. Look out for bones, feathers or fur lying around the entrance.

Flattened undergrowth
In the spring, young cubs dig holes and play near their earth. The undergrowth is flattened and the ground disturbed. The cubs chew sticks, roots or anything else near the earth entrance. These are covered with tiny, pointed tooth marks.

Droppings
Fox droppings are very black and often contain lots of hair or feathers. They are usually left in very visible places, such as on a stone, log or high ground.

8–10 cm

Eyeshine
Fox eyes are highly reflective and glow with a blue-white colour when they are caught in bright lights such as car headlamps. These can be seen up to 400 m away. Often only the eyes are visible, while the rest of the animal is completely hidden in the darkness.

Smell
Foxes have a powerful smell that is unlike any other European mammal. Their scent lingers for several hours after they have disappeared, particularly around the earth.

Footprints
Unlike cats, fox claws are non-retractable and can be clearly seen on the footprint. Fox prints are more oval-shaped than those of a dog.

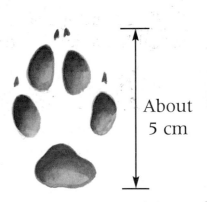

About 5 cm

Night calls
Loud, long calls at night are a good sign that foxes are nearby.

Hairs
Look out for rusty-red hairs caught on twigs and fences.

Glossary

ambush To attack by surprise.

camouflage The colour or pattern of some animals that helps them blend in with their surroundings and makes them hard to see.

canine teeth Long, sharp teeth towards the front of the mouth, used for killing and tearing meat.

carrion The body of a dead animal that is eaten by another animal.

distemper A very infectious disease that usually affects dogs.

dog A male fox.

dominant The strongest animal in a territory or group.

earth The den of a fox.

habitat The area where an animal or plant naturally lives.

litter A group of young animals born at the same time from the same mother.

nocturnal An animal that sleeps during the day and is active at night.

non-retractable Claws that stay in one position, and cannot be drawn back like those of a cat.

omnivore An animal that eats both meat and plants.

predator An animal that kills and eats other animals.

prey An animal that is killed and eaten by other animals. This word is also used as a verb. 'To prey on' means 'to hunt', or 'take as prey'.

rabies A deadly disease that affects all mammals, including humans.

rodents Small animals such as rats, mice or voles with sharp, gnawing teeth.

stalking Creeping silently and slowly, trying to catch prey without being seen.

suckle When a mother allows her young to drink milk from her teats.

territory An area that an animal defends against others of the same species.

urban To do with a town or city.

vixen A female fox.

Finding Out More

Other books to read

Animal Classification: A Guide to Vertebrates by Polly Goodman (Wayland, 2004)

Animal Sanctuary by John Bryant (Open Gate Press, 1999)

Animal Young: Mammals by Rod Theodorou (Heinemann, 2000)

Crafty Canines: Coyotes, Foxes and Wolves by Phyllis J Perry (Watts, 2000)

Foxes: Wild Canines by Jalma Barrett & Larry Allan (Blackbirch Press, 2000)

Collins Nature Guides: Garden Wildlife of Britain and Europe by Michael Chinery (Collins Natural History, 1997)

Country Foxes by Hugh Kolb (Whittet, 1996)

Life Cycles: Cats and Other Mammals by Sally Morgan (Chrysalis, 2003)

Life Cycle of a Dog by Angela Royston (Heinemann, 2001)

Living with Urban Wildlife by John Bryant (Open Gate Press, 2002)

Natural World: Wolf by Michael Leach (Wayland, 2002)

New Encyclopedia of Mammals by David Macdonald (OUP, 2006)

Urban Foxes by Stephen Harris and Phil Baker (Whittet, 2000)

The Wayland Book of Common British Mammals by Shirley Thompson (Wayland, 2000)

What's the Difference?: Mammals by Stephen Savage (Wayland, 2002)

Wild Britain: Woodlands; Parks & Gardens; Meadows by R. & L. Spilsbury (Heinemann, 2002)

Worldlife Library: Foxes by David Macdonald (Voyageur Press, 2000)

Organisations to contact

Countryside Foundation for Education
PO Box 8
Hebden Bridge HX7 5YJ
www.countrysidefoundation.org.uk
Training and teaching materials
to help people understand the
countryside and its problems.

The Mammal Society
2B Inworth Street
London SW11 3EP
www.abdn.ac.uk/mammal/
Promotes the study and conservation
of British mammals.

Wildlife Watch
The Kiln, Mather Road
Newark
NG24 1WT
www.wildlifewatch.org.uk
The junior branch of the Wildlife Trusts, a
network of local Wildlife Trusts caring for
nearly 2,500 nature reserves, from rugged
coastline to urban wildlife havens, protecting
a huge number of habitats and species.

Index

Page numbers in **bold** refer to a photograph or illustration.

badgers 8, 20

birds **16**, **17**, **26**

birth 8, 28

camouflage **14**

communication 4, 10, 23, 29

cubs 5, 7, **8**, **9**, **10**, **11**, 23, 24, **28**

deserts 4, 7

disease 27

dogs 4, 5, **6–7**, 13, **24**

droppings 13, **29**

earth 8, **9**, 10, 11, 24, **29**

farms 4, **11**, 12, **17** **26**

fighting 4, **11**, **12**, **22**, 23

food 6, **10**, 12, **15**, **16–21**, 27, **28**

foxes

Arctic 4, 7

bat-eared **6–7**

fennec 7

grey 4

fur **4**, 7, 15, 29

habitat 4, 7, **12–15**

hearing 5, 7, 8, 18

heat 7, 8, 15, 16

hunting 6, 8, 11, 12, 15, **18–19**, 24

insects 6, **16**

map of distribution **4**

mice **16**, 17, 18, 20, 21, 26

myths and folk tales 19, 24

pets 7, **27**

play-fighting **11**

predators 6, 24

prey 5, 7, 18, **19**, 20, 26

scent-marking **13**

seasons 8, 15, 16, 17, 22, 28, 29

sight 5, 8, 18, 28

smell 8, 10, 13, 15, 18

teeth **5**, **11**, 18

territory **12**, **13**, 28, 29

towns and cities 4, 8, 12, 14, **15**, **20**, **21**, 24, **25**, 27

traffic 21, **25**

vixens 5, 8, 9, **10**, 13, 22, **23**

voles **16**, 17

wolves **6**, 7, 24

woodlands 12, **14**